Earth Day

Willma Willis Gore

Reading Consultant:

Michael P. French, Ph.D.,
Bowling Green State University

—Best Holiday Books—

ENSLOW PUBLISHERS, INC.

Bloy St. and Ramsey Ave.   P.O. Box 38
Box 777   Aldershot
Hillside, N.J. 07205   Hants GU12 6BP
U.S.A.   U.K.

> ## *In memory of Charles*

Library of Congress Cataloging-in-Publication Data

Gore, Willma Willis.
    Earth day / Willma Willis Gore.
       p. cm. — (Best holiday books)
    Includes index.
    Summary: Discusses the concern for the environment that produced
the original Earth Day and describes the activities that accompany
its continuing celebration in the United States and around the
world.
    ISBN 0-89490-380-2
    1. Earth Day—Juvenile literature. 2. Environmental policy—
United States—Juvenile literature. 3. Environmental protection—
United States—Juvenile literature. [1. Earth Day.
2. Environmental protection.] I. Title. II. Series.
HC110.E5G66 1992
    333.7—dc20
                                   91-43199
                                      CIP
                                      AC

Printed in the United States of America

10 9 8 7 6 5 4 3 2 1

Illustration credits:

Bonnie Rhodes, p. 21; Earth Day, U.S.A., p. 14; NASA, National Aeronautics and
Space Administration, pp. 4, 17; National Arbor Day Foundation, p. 24; Public
Communications, University of California, Davis, p. 37; Thomas Yen, p. 27; Willma
Willis Gore, pp. 8, 12, 20, 23, 29, 31, 35, 38, 40.

Cover illustration: Charlott Nathan

Contents

Earth seen from space looks like a beautiful blue marble.

What Is Earth Day?

We celebrate Earth Day on April 22 every year. Earth Day is a holiday for everyone in the world. It is the day we honor our planet Earth.

Earth is one of the planets in the solar system. It is the only one we know of that has people, birds, and animals. It is the only one with oceans, rain, and trees. Everything around us is the earth's environment.

On Earth Day children, teachers, and parents talk about the earth. Television stations show pictures. Magazines and newspapers print stories. They tell ways the earth's environment is in danger. They tell ways we can help the earth.

Many cities have Earth Day parades. People walk or ride in the parades. Some wear "Save the Earth" T-shirts.

School children write stories about how to help the earth. Some draw pictures that show ways to help. They print slogans on their pictures. Slogans are words that tell about an idea. The slogans may say "Love Our Birds" or "Save the Elephants."

Many parks have celebrations on Earth Day. Visitors get free booklets and stories and posters. A poster is a large picture. The children learn how our environment is in danger.

One danger to our environment is pollution. Waste paper, empty cans, and used bottles can be forms of pollution. Plastic wrap and sacks also can be pollution. Dumps do not have enough space for this waste.

Another kind of pollution is unsafe materials in the air. Many unsafe materials come from cars using gasoline. Some people try to drive less. They join carpools. This means they ride to work or school together. Driving fewer cars saves gas. Less pollution gets into the air.

Some factory owners do not seem to care about the environment. After they make a product they have unsafe materials left. Sometimes these are put on the land. Sometimes they are put into streams. The unsafe materials pollute the earth's land and water.

On Earth Day people learn new ways to stop pollution. They learn that some things we throw away can be recycled. This means they can be used again to make new products.

These children are proud to be Native Americans. Their ancestors cared for the earth and did not pollute the land or the water.

The First Earth Day

Long ago Native Americans called the earth "our mother." The earth took care of them like parents care for their children. The earth gave them everything they needed.

The Native Americans took only what they could use. They did not pollute the streams. They did not waste food, water, or trees. The Native Americans said the earth does not belong to the people. People belong to the earth. They believed animals and people are the children of the earth. They took care of the environment.

In 1607 the first colonists from England came to America. They built villages. Every year more and more new people came to America. Not all of these people took good care of the environment. This made the Native Americans sad. As years passed many others felt sad too. They knew we needed to take better care of our environment.

Famous people showed they cared about the environment. James Audubon was a painter. He made beautiful pictures of birds. His pictures taught people to love and care for birds.

Henry David Thoreau was a writer. He wrote about ponds, streams, and trees. His stories helped people love these things in nature.

John Muir studied the California mountains. He spent most of his life in these mountains. His ideas helped people care for the mountains and other beautiful places. Two of these places are Yosemite and Sequoia national parks.

Rachel Carson was a scientist who studied pollution. She wrote books. She told how some things make animals and people sick. She helped stop the use of them.

These people helped in their own ways but the environment was still in danger. The earth needed more help.

Gaylord Nelson was born on June 4, 1916, in Clear Lake, Wisconsin. As a young child, he loved nature. He studied ways to help the earth.

When he grew up, he studied law. He was a state senator for ten years. He was governor of his state for four years. While he was governor, he helped young people learn about the environment. He said, "People who learn to love Earth will take care of it."

While he was governor, his state bought one million acres of forest land. The state turned this land into parks. The parks gave the wildlife a safe place to live. Many families learned about the environment in these parks.

In 1962 he was elected United States senator. As senator, Nelson worked for the environment. He and other senators passed laws to make cars use less gasoline.

June Lake in the High Sierra of California attracts many visitors. Gaylord Nelson helped people learn about the importance of nature in places like this.

Nelson talked to important people about the environment. One of these people was John F. Kennedy, President of the United States. In 1963 they traveled together to tell people about dangers to the environment. Still, not everybody understood.

Then Nelson thought of a new way to help the earth. He got the idea from young people at colleges. Students often got together for teach-ins. Teach-ins are meetings where many people share ideas.

Nelson said, "We'll have a teach-in about the earth's environment." He invited others to help. One of the people he invited to help was Denis Hayes. Like Nelson, Hayes believed everyone should help our planet.

Nelson and the people helping him talked to the governors of states. They telephoned mayors of cities and school leaders. They got help from newspapers and magazines. All agreed to hold a celebration for the earth. They

Gaylord Nelson founded Earth Day in 1970. He is called the father of Earth Day.

decided to call it Earth Day. The first Earth Day celebration was on April 22, 1970.

Millions of people across the United States celebrated. One thousand cities and towns celebrated. Children in 10,000 grade schools and high schools joined in. They drew "Save the Earth" posters. They made banners to put up on streets. They marched in parades. Families planted trees on Earth Day. Students and workers rode bicycles instead of driving cars. Earth Day has been held on April 22 ever since.

Gaylord Nelson is known as the father of Earth Day. He still works to help the environment. He is chairman of Earth Day USA. His office is in Washington, D.C. The office for the world's celebrations of Earth Day is in Victoria, Canada.

Earth Day Today

After the first Earth Day, people wrote to government leaders. They asked, "What can we do to help?" Earth Day leaders sent ideas to everyone who asked. Many people got busy helping. New people across the United States celebrate Earth Day each year. People in more than 140 countries also celebrate it.

Earth Day celebrations make more people think about the environment. They talk about the environment with each other. They talk to government leaders. Many leaders listen to the people.

Nelson's state, Wisconsin, made rules for its schools. In Wisconsin every school child must study the environment. The studies begin in kindergarten. After the first Earth Day, more states made the same rule.

Years ago, people in the United States used a material called DDT. It killed insects. People did not know it also killed birds and wildlife. Now people everywhere know about DDT. The government leaders made everybody stop using it.

Some factories dumped waste into rivers. The waste polluted the water. This pollution

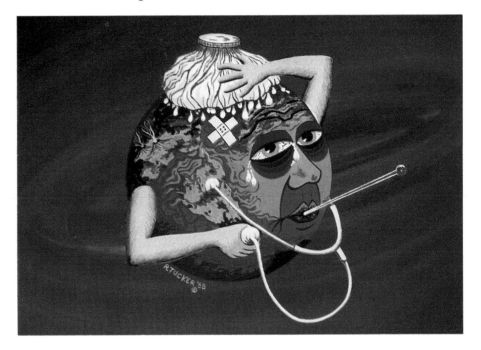

We know the earth needs better care. Years ago, some people polluted the earth and water with DDT and other unsafe things.

made the water unsafe to drink. The government leaders made rules to stop water pollution. They made rules to save forests for parks and wildlife.

Many good things happened after the first Earth Day. But the environment still needs help.

Gaylord Nelson says young people are the helpers of the future. At school they learn about the earth and the solar system. They learn about air, water, and trees. This teaches them how to care for the earth's environment.

How Schools Celebrate Earth Day

Children in schools across the United States celebrate Earth Day every year.

One city had a poster contest for school children. Each child made a "Save the Earth" poster. Their teachers took the posters to the city's zoo. They hung the posters beside the animal cages. The zoo had a big celebration on Earth Day. Hundreds of people came. The school children visited the zoo. Each one found his or her poster. Some got to tell about their posters on the radio.

One class studied the environment before Earth Day. They learned about trees. They knew that trees are homes for birds and butterflies. All

All the entries in one city's poster contest were displayed at their zoo on Earth Day.

knew trees make shade. The teacher explained more about trees. All paper for school work comes from trees. Paper for boxes, magazines, and newspapers comes from trees.

Trees also fight air pollution. Trees do not breathe like people, but they clean the air. They need some of the gasses in the air that are bad for people. They give out oxygen that people need.

OXYGEN

O₂

CARBON DIOXIDE

CO₂

Some children wanted to buy a tree for the school. The teacher said they could earn the money by recycling. Waste glass, cans, and paper can be recycled. Used glass jars and bottles can be melted. Melted glass is made into new bottles and jars. Aluminum cans can be melted and made into new cans. Old newspapers can be made into boxes.

The teacher gave each boy and girl a big sack. The children picked up paper and cans in the school yard. They brought used glass, cans, and newspapers from home.

The next day they went on a field trip. They took their sacks of waste to a recycling center. A worker weighed the glass and the cans. He paid money to the class.

The class used the money to buy an elm tree. On Earth Day the children planted the tree in the school yard.

At one school, children made Earth Day pictures. They used old crayons and leaves from the park. They shaved the old crayons into tiny pieces. They put the pieces and the leaves between sheets of wax paper. Then the children ran a warm iron over the paper. The leaves and crayon shavings made a pretty picture. The teacher hung the pictures in the classroom. Parents and other visitors saw the pictures on Earth Day.

These children are helping the earth by picking up litter. Everyone can work to save the earth.

Actor Eddie Albert and a friend celebrate the earth by planting a tree.

How the World Celebrates Earth Day

Every year people find new ways to celebrate Earth Day. They celebrate in towns, cities, and parks.

In California, a Girl Scout troop played earth ball. The earth ball is like a giant balloon. It is painted to show all the countries on the earth. Teams of Girl Scouts lie on the ground. They raise their feet up in the air. The Scout leader puts the ball on their feet. The team that keeps the ball up longest wins.

A children's theater in Rhode Island put on a play. It was a story called "End of the World Cafe." Mother Earth was in the play. She hired a detective. A detective is a person who finds unknown facts. Mother Earth wanted to find out why anyone wanted to kill her. In the play, the detective found the killers. They were the polluters.

A big Earth Day parade was held in Honolulu, Hawaii. The parade had special rules. People could walk or run in the parade. They could ride bicycles. But no gasoline-burning cars could be in the parade.

Only cars that do not pollute the air could be in it. Some cars used the sun's energy. This is called solar energy. Solar cells on top of the car make electricity from the sun's energy. This energy makes the car run.

Electric cars were in the parade. Their power comes from batteries. Batteries store electricity. After a while, batteries run out of power. Then the driver doesn't buy gasoline. He gets his batteries recharged. This means he fills up with electric power instead of gasoline. Many people saw the Honolulu parade. They learned about kinds of energy that do not pollute.

In Maryland, hundreds of people had fun on Earth Day. Along the shores of Chesapeake Bay they planted trees. They planted marsh grass to help the birds. They planted "DON'T DUMP" signs. These tell others not to dump trash. This helps keep the environment clean.

At a Washington zoo, elephants helped celebrate Earth Day. A worker taught them how

This car is a solar car named the "Racin' Raysun." It gets its energy only from the sun.

to crush aluminum cans with their feet. Many people saw this. They learned it is good to recycle cans.

In California another zoo had an Earth Day celebration. A girl dressed in a beaver costume shook hands with visitors. The beaver's name was "Bubbles." She told boys and girls that beavers need clean water. She said, "Take trash home when you picnic near the water. This keeps the beavers' homes clean. It also keeps pollution out of the river."

A radio reporter made the children laugh. He spoke to a little tree. Then he made believe the tree answered. It said, "Take me home. Plant me in your yard."

Children drew pictures at tables near the animal cages. At one table they learned about rock painting. Native Americans painted on rocks to tell stories.

Children put one hand on a grocery bag. Each drew around his or her hand with a marker. The hand print was like the Native Americans' rock

"Bubbles" the Beaver greeted zoo visitors and reminded them to use water wisely.

painting. Children used the grocery bags to carry papers and prizes.

At beaches in Texas, California, and Oregon, families celebrated Earth Day. They picked up trash on the beaches. They made the shores look beautiful again.

On Vancouver Island, Canada, Boy Scouts worked together. A forest was about to be cut down. On Earth Day the Scouts dug up the baby trees in the forest. They replanted the little trees in a safe place.

Children in Japan learned about the world's rain forests. These are places where rain falls every day. Rain forests have millions of trees and other plants growing close together. Many kinds of wildlife live only in these forests. Some people are cutting and burning trees in the rain forest. This destroys the home of the wildlife.

These children in Japan wanted to help save the rain forests. They found cans and newspapers to recycle. They got money for them. On Earth Day they sent the money to the

International Children's Rain Forest Program. The money paid for forty acres of rain forest in Central America. Now this forest belongs to the Children's Rain Forest Program. Nobody can cut or burn it.

These children collected newspapers and brought them to a recycling center. Their work helped save trees.

Famous rock star Paul McCartney was on a world tour. On Earth Day he was in Brazil. His band gave a concert. He told the listeners the concert was in honor of the environment. He gave money from the concert to help the environment.

Every Day Earth Day

On Earth Day's twenty-first birthday there was a big celebration. Gaylord Nelson and other leaders chose a new slogan. It was "Make Every Day Earth Day."

Many people liked this idea. They do not wait until April 22. They work to help the environment every day.

One of these people is Andy Lipkis of Los Angeles. When Andy was fifteen years old, he learned about pollution. He found that polluted air killed 40,000 trees each year. These trees were dying in the forests around his city.

He and his friends found a place in the city without buildings. They planted trees there that grow in polluted air. That was the start of a club called TreePeople. Anyone who wants to help the environment can join TreePeople. They call themselves "Treeps."

People in the United States use lots of plastic. Each person uses about 190 pounds of plastic every year. Most of this is boxes and sacks. When the plastic is thrown away, it takes up lots of dump space. Plastic in dumps stays there. It may be there for 500 years.

A high school boy in North Carolina was sad about waste plastic. Plastic cups and plates were used in his school's cafeteria. He talked to his friends and teachers. Now all the waste plastic in the cafeteria is saved. It is recycled. The recycling company turns the waste plastic into rulers and lunch trays. These can be used many times. This saves space in the dump.

Ohio college students had a picnic without using plastic. First they cooked waffles. Then they used the waffles as plates and bowls. They put food on the waffle plates. Then they ate the

It is important to recycle plastic. When plastic is thrown away, it may
stay in a dump up to 500 years!

waffles. Nothing was wasted. No plastic went to the dump after the picnic.

Many families join "adopt a highway" programs. Each family chooses part of a highway to keep clean. Parents and children pick up trash beside the highway. The family's name is on a sign beside the highway. It says: "This highway adopted by the Jones Family."

Another family wanted to help stop air pollution. They sold their cars on Earth Day. Now they ride bicycles or buses to their city jobs. They have a bike with two seats. It has a trailer for their baby. They also carry food and packages in the trailer.

Everyone can help the environment. Many children do things to help. They give reports in school about how they help the earth.

Saving water is a way everyone can help. Big lakes and rivers make us think we have lots of water. But many people live where there is not enough water.

One boy told how he saves water when he brushes his teeth. First he gets his toothbrush wet. Then he turns off the water faucet while he brushes.

The city of Davis, California has forty-six miles of bicycle paths. Lots of people there ride bicycles to work and school.

His family also keeps a bottle of water in the refrigerator. No one has to let the faucet run to get a cool drink.

Another student told how her family recycles grocery bags. She saves and folds them at home. When the family shops, they take the empty bags. Their grocery store pays five cents for each bag.

Take paper grocery bags back to the store for recycling. Next time, take a canvas shopping bag.

Her family also saves paper in the kitchen. They don't use paper towels. They use a cloth to wipe up spills and to dry hands. This keeps paper towels out of their city's dump.

Many children bring their lunches to school. One puts his sandwich in a plastic box. The box can be used again and again. This keeps paper and plastic wrap out of the dump.

One kind of plastic is the holder for soft drink cans. These holders are called six-pack rings. The rings are very strong. A bird or animal may put its head through a ring. Some animals can't swallow with rings around their necks. The rings can keep birds from flying. Children can cut the circles apart before throwing them away.

There are many ways to celebrate Earth Day every day. Recycle paper, cans, glass, and plastic. Plant trees and care for them. Ask drivers to carpool.

Many cities place containers on parking lots where you can take your glass to recycle.

Remember the Native Americans. Like them, we should take only what we need from the earth. We should not waste anything in our environment. That is the best way to make every day Earth Day.

Glossary

adopt—To choose to take care of someone or something.

aluminum—A light metal. It is used to make many things, including drink cans.

Brazil—A country in South America that has many rain forests.

carpool—Several people riding in one car.

chairman (also called chair or chairperson)—A person who is in charge of a meeting or group.

dump—A place to store waste; sometimes called a landfill.

DDT—A material used to kill insects (dichloro-diphenyl-trichloroethane).

electric car—A car that runs on energy stored in batteries.

environment—The people, animals, plants, natural, and man-made things around us.

field trip—A trip to visit a place away from school.

governor—A person chosen by voters to lead a state.

marsh grass—A grass that grows in wet places.

oxygen—A gas in the air that people and animals need to breathe.

pollution—Any unclean, unsafe, or ugly material in the environment.

radio reporter—A person who talks about news and events on the radio.

rain forest—A thick forest of trees that gets a lot of rain.

recycle—To use again and again.

rock painting—Pictures and symbols painted on rocks.

senator—A person chosen by voters to be a leader in his or her state or nation.

shaving—A tiny piece of material cut from a larger piece.

six-pack rings—Plastic rings used to hold cans of soft drinks together.

slogan—A few words chosen to explain a big idea.

solar cells—The parts of a solar battery that change sunlight into electricity.

solar energy—Energy from the sun.

solar system—The sun and the nine planets, (including Earth), the moons, and the asteroids that orbit the sun.

teach-in—A meeting of many people to learn new ideas.

Index